DAILY LIFE IN A
PLAINS INDIAN VILLAGE 1868

MICHAEL BAD HAND TERRY

Heinemann
LIBRARY

First published in Great Britain
by Heinemann Library, Halley Court, Jordan Hill, Oxford, OX2 8EJ
a division of Reed Educational and Professional
Publishing Limited

Heinemann is a registered trademark of Reed Educational
and Professional Publishing Limited

OXFORD MELBOURNE AUCKLAND
JOHANNESBURG BLANTYRE GABORONE
IBADAN PORTSMOUTH (NH) USA CHICAGO

British Library Cataloguing in Publication Data

Terry, Michael
Daily life in a plains Indian village
1. Indians of North America – Great Plains – Social
conditions – Juvenile literature 2. Indians of North
America
– Great Plains – History – Juvenile literature
I. Title
978'.00497
ISBN 0431042403

Printed in Hong Kong

Conceived and produced by Breslich & Foss Ltd, London
Series Editor: Laura Wilson
Art Director: Nigel Osborne
Design: Phil Richardson
Photography: Miki Slingsby

CONTENTS

WHO WERE THE PLAINS INDIANS?

Above: *Plains Indian council meeting, 1878*

Over 14,000 years ago, the ancestors of the Plains Indians migrated from Asia to North America where many of them settled in the upper Mississippi River and Great Lakes areas. Displaced from their land by Europeans who came to settle in the east, they moved to the plains of central America (*see map opposite*).

Most of the Plains Indians were nomadic, which means that they were not farmers who stayed in one place and raised crops on the land, but hunter-gatherers who moved about, getting their food by killing buffalo from the large herds that grazed the prairies and by trading goods with other tribes.

In the mid 1800s, immigrants and settlers began to come from the east, travelling westward in covered waggons, and claiming some of the Plains Indian territory for themselves. The US army began to build forts in these areas. Relations between the Plains Indians and the white settlers grew increasingly tense and eventually the massacre of an Indian village occurred. This marked the beginning of over 30 years of war between the Plains Indians and the US army. Within five years of the Sioux and Cheyenne victory at the Battle of the Little Bighorn in 1876 the old time nomadic, buffalo-hunting culture was gone.

Below: *War played an important part in Plains Indian culture, as shown in this painting called "Indian Warfare" by Frederic Remington.*

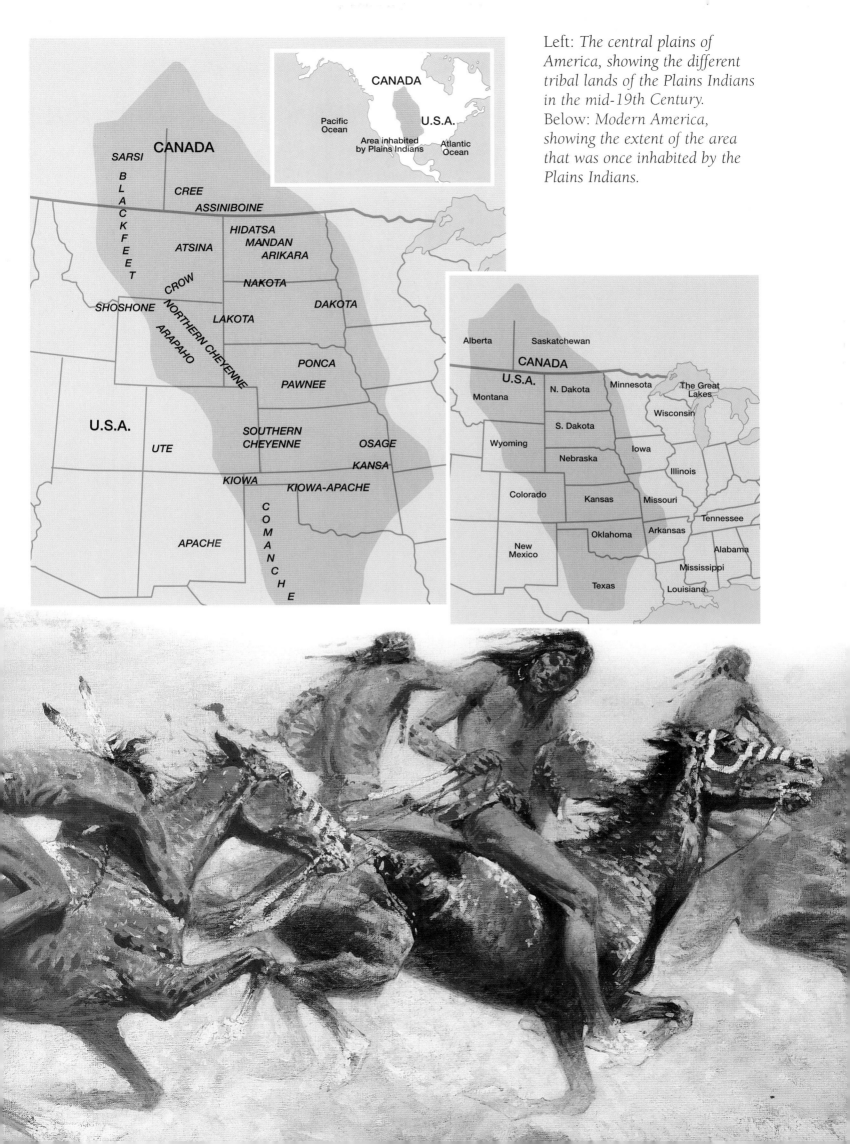

Left: *The central plains of America, showing the different tribal lands of the Plains Indians in the mid-19th Century.*
Below: *Modern America, showing the extent of the area that was once inhabited by the Plains Indians.*

Map 1 (central plains, mid-19th century):

CANADA

Pacific Ocean

U.S.A.

Area inhabited by Plains Indians

Atlantic Ocean

CANADA

SARSI
BLACKFEET
CREE
ASSINIBOINE
HIDATSA
MANDAN
ARIKARA
ATSINA
NAKOTA
CROW
DAKOTA
SHOSHONE
LAKOTA
NORTHERN CHEYENNE
ARAPAHO
PONCA
PAWNEE
U.S.A.
UTE
SOUTHERN CHEYENNE
OSAGE
KANSA
KIOWA
KIOWA-APACHE
COMANCHE
APACHE

Map 2 (modern America):

Alberta
Saskatchewan
CANADA
U.S.A.
Montana
N. Dakota
Minnesota
The Great Lakes
Wisconsin
S. Dakota
Wyoming
Iowa
Nebraska
Illinois
Colorado
Kansas
Missouri
Tennessee
Oklahoma
Arkansas
Alabama
New Mexico
Mississippi
Texas
Louisiana

THE PLAINS INDIAN TRIBES

Although there were around 30 different tribes of Plains Indians, their total population was never more than 200,000 people. All the tribes spoke different languages, although some of them had similar words and sounds. Large tribes like the Sioux were divided into sub-tribes (the Lakota, Nakota and Dakota Sioux), which, in turn, were divided into smaller units called hunting bands. These people lived together and could not marry anyone within the same band. When a man married, he usually went to live with his wife's band.

Right: *Northern Cheyenne warrior. His shirt and leggings are trimmed with human hair to show that he is a war party leader.*

The Cheyenne
The Cheyenne moved onto the Plains in the mid 1700s. In the 1820s, they divided into two groups, the Northern Cheyenne, who lived in the territories that are now Montana and Wyoming, and the Southern Cheyenne, who lived in what are now Nebraska, Colorado, Kansas and Oklahoma. The total Cheyenne population numbered around 3,000 people. From the 1830s onwards, the Cheyenne were friendly with the Lakota Sioux tribe. Their traditional enemies included the Ute, Pawnee, Crow and Blackfeet.

The Lakota Sioux
The Lakota were one of the last tribal groups to move onto the Plains, but they quickly adapted to their new lifestyle. They were a large and powerful tribe of about 12,000 people, who were very influential in both Plains Indian culture and politics.

Right: *This Lakota Sioux warrior carries a war party leader's lance and stone club. His headdress is made of ermine skins, buffalo horns and eagle feathers.*

Left: *Southern Cheyenne Dogman. His headdress, rattle, paint design and sash show that he is a member of the Dog Society, a police and military organisation which eventually became an independent band within the Cheyenne nation.*

Above: *Southern Cheyenne woman. Holding her saddle and a painted buffalo robe, she is wearing her best clothes for a tribal celebration.*

Right and centre: *Blackfeet "Grizzly Bear Man".*
Below: *This Crow man is holding a combination pipe and tomahawk. His clothes show his exploits in battle: he has captured a gun and led war parties and horse-stealing raids.*

The Crow

Numbering around 4,000, the Crow were a very artistic people who lived along the Yellowstone River. Surrounded by their traditional enemies – the Blackfeet, Cheyenne, Arapaho and Sioux – the Crow became the allies of the white settlers.

Below: *Blackfeet chief.*

The Blackfeet

Like the Sioux, the Blackfeet were divided into three main groups. Numbering around 18,000 people, they dominated southern Alberta, Canada and western Montana. This area had plenty of grass and water, and was one of the last places that herds of buffalo could be found. The Blackfeet fought against almost all the other tribes, with no allies except for the Sarsi (a small tribe of around 800 people) and sometimes the Atsina (3,000 people).

The Blackfeet had a Braves' Society that chose two men every year to serve as "Grizzly Bear Men". These men had to be fierce warriors who fought like grizzly bears, always charging at the enemy. When going into battle and on ceremonial occasions, they wore bear fur arm bands, bear claw necklaces, a bear fur belt and a special headdress made from two grizzly claws.

Far right: *This Blackfeet woman is holding a travois. The wooden A-frame platform was placed on the back of a dog or horse and loaded up with baggage. When the animal moved forward the two poles were dragged along behind. The Plains Indians used these platforms to transport their belongings.*

THE HORSE

Between 1.5 million and 600,000 years ago, the ancestors of modern horses migrated from Asia to the North American continent, travelling across the Bering Land Bridge which joined the two land masses during this time. However, they became extinct in the New World, and were unknown to the Native peoples until they were re-introduced into Mexico by the Spaniards in the 1500s. As these horses were traded and captured, they began to move northwards throughout America, and by the the mid 1700s, most of the Plains Indians used horses.

The arrival of the horse transformed the lives of the Plains Indians, who had previously relied on dogs to carry their belongings as they moved around. As horses can transport far heavier loads than dogs, the Plains Indians were able to make themselves bigger tipis and keep larger supplies of food. They were also able to travel further and faster than ever before. Children became used to horses from an early age, and both boys and girls were taught to ride.

Below: *A man's saddle. The buffalo-hide pad is stuffed with antelope or buffalo hair. The stirrups are made of green cottonwood and covered with rawhide. The saddle blanket, made from the skin of a mountain lion, would have been a prized item.*

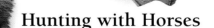

Hunting with Horses

Although buffalo are large, heavy animals, they gallop fast, and hunting them on foot usually involved stampeding them over a cliff and taking those animals killed in the fall. The arrival of the horse meant that hunters could chase the buffalo herds, and each man could pick out one or two animals and shoot them. A fast and obedient horse was essential for success in hunting.

Horses in Warfare

A rich family might own as many as 30 horses, but only one or two would be good enough to be ridden into battle. Success for a warrior or a hunter depended on owning a fast, well-trained and brave horse. Good horsemanship was also very important. In battle especially, being able to stay on the horse's back meant staying alive, while falling – or being dragged – off a horse meant almost certain death. The best riders could rescue fallen comrades by lifting them onto their galloping horses in the thick of battle. They could also protect themselves from bullets and arrows by slipping round to one side of their horse and hanging there to avoid being hit.

Left: *A scarf or banner tied onto the horse's bridle showed that it had been ridden into battle before.*

Above: *An Indian family moving camp. One of the horses pulls a travois laden with belongings.*

Right: *Plains Indians either made their own bridles from plaited buffalo hide or hair. Sometimes they used leather bridles with metal bits, bought from white traders.*

THE FAMILY

The year is 1868, and the Northern Cheyenne warrior Real Bird and his family live on the plains of south-eastern Montana. Families are very important to the Plains Indian culture, and each of the members has a particular part to play. A boy's success as a warrior and hunter, and a girl's skill as a homemaker and craftswoman, are both vital for the continued well-being of each family, and therefore of the tribe as a whole.

Above: *Timber Leader, the grandfather, looks after the family's spiritual needs. He has been a great warrior, and young men come to him for advice and to listen to his stories of past battles. Brave Heart Woman, the grandmother, is an expert homemaker and craftswoman. She is now passing on these skills to her granddaughters. She watches Real Bird's wives to make sure that they are doing their work properly.*

Polygamy

Real Bird is a polygamist, which means that he has more than one wife. Most of the men in his village have two or three wives, and very rich men have as many as eight. It was common for a man to marry two or three sisters.

One reason for Plains Indians to be polygamous was the war-like nature of their society. Hunting accidents and deaths in battle meant that there were always fewer men than women.

Women usually married aged 14 or 15, and men some time in their twenties. Families were not encouraged to have many children. It was hard to find food on the plains and too many people would have meant starvation for everyone.

In addition to their other roles, wives contributed to the family's wealth by preparing buffalo hides for trade.

Below: Real Bird's two wives are Sees the Berries Woman (left) and Pretty Plume Woman (right). Sees the Berries Woman, a Southern Cheyenne, is the senior wife. She has a son, Rides the Herd (below right), aged ten, and a daughter, Does Well (centre), aged eight. Pretty Plume Woman's daughter, Two Whistles (below centre), is six years old.

Left:
Real Bird, the father, is an experienced hunter and provides well for his family. He is also a good trader, and raises fine horses for racing and hunting.

Above: *Real Bird's eldest child, Eagle that Sings, is the son of his first wife, who is now dead. Now 17 years old, Eagle that Sings must spend several years going on horse-stealing raids and war parties before he owns enough horses to be able to marry. Unlike his father, Eagle that Sings prefers the new style of dress, using some of the white man's clothes.*

THE VILLAGE

Almost all of the Plains Indians fed themselves by hunting, not farming, which meant that they needed to move from place to place. Each tribe was divided into several smaller groups called bands. Apart from certain times of year, when all the bands came together for ceremonies and celebrations, they lived separately. Each band had to be small enough to move about fairly quickly and not use up too much food. It also had to be large enough to have enough men for a hunting party or to defend the village from enemy attack.

Right: *Setting up camp. Real Bird and the rest of his party have arrived in a new place. When the men have given the horses water, they relax and smoke their pipes, while the women set up the tipis (see page 16) and prepare the afternoon meal. After this, the children are allowed to play while Real Bird and his wives visit friends and other family members.*

Wickiups

Family tipis are often crowded places. In order to have their own space to sit and chat with friends, young warriors like Eagle that Sings build themselves temporary brush-covered huts called wickiups.

Above: *The small bands who travel together usually set up their tipis next to a river, if they can find one. When the whole tribe meet together for a ceremony, or if they suspect that there are enemies in the area, they lay the tipis out in concentric circles. Tipis belonging to chiefs and warrior societies are usually placed at the centre of the village.*

Right: *When travelling, the family packs their food and tools in carrying-cases called parfleches, which are made of folded and decorated buffalo hide.*

Travelling

Real Bird and his family are packed up and ready to move camp. They are waiting for the other families in their band, because travelling in a small family group is not safe.

During the winter, the Real Bird family and their band live in one camp for several months. First the whole tribe has a large buffalo hunt so that there are enough hides for a good supply of robes to trade and keep them warm, and plenty of meat dried and stored for the coming months.

In the spring, summer and autumn, the band moves camp every few days. When travelling, they move slowly, covering eight to 15 miles per day until they come to a place with fresh water, wood for their fires and plenty of good grass for the horses.

SETTING UP A TIPI

P lains Indians needed strong but lightweight dwellings that were easy to carry and erect. Buffalo-hide tipis were ideal for their nomadic lifestyle. In the days before horses, when the Plains Indians had only dogs to pull their loads, their tipis measured 2.5 to 3.5 metres across. With the arrival of horses, which could carry more weight than dogs could manage, the tipis increased in size to about 4 to 5 metres across. Traditionally, the family tipi and its contents and furnishings belonged to the women, and it was their job both to transport it and to set it up on arrival at a new camp.

Left: *Tools for setting up a tipi. The bag, a US Cavalry feedbag contains wooden pegs to hold down the tipi cover and an elk-horn hammer to knock them into the ground. The thin sticks are "lacing pins".*

Ceremonial Tipis

Besides family tipis there were also several larger tipis in each village where meetings were held. These could be up to 30 metres across, and were either made out of several buffalo-hide tipi covers stretched between poles in a circle or semi-circle, or involved two large tipis which were set up facing each other, with a piece of hide stretched between them.

1 *The frame of the tipi is made of either three or four wooden poles, tied together with a rope. Once the frame is up, extra poles are leant against it. Pretty Plume Woman ties strips of cloth to the tops of the poles to show which way the wind is blowing.*

2 *The remaining poles are added to the frame by leaning them against the central notch. When all the poles are in place, the women unpack the hide cover. Buffalo hide covers can weigh up to 75kg, so the two women always work together.*

3 *The women fold the heavy tipi cover into a triangle and tie it to a pole that is placed on the ground. This last pole is then lifted into position at the back of the tipi, opposite where the tent flaps will be.*

4 The women unfurl the cover
(left), and pull it around the
framework of poles.

Smoke flap pocket

Smoke flap

Above: *Buffalo hide tipi cover.*
Two semi-circular pieces are
sometimes cut out for the door.
Below: *A finished tipi.*

Making a Tipi Cover

Tipis can be patched when they wear out, but industrious women
like Sees the Berries Woman and Pretty Plume Woman replace their
tipi at least every other year. They need eight to 20 tanned buffalo
hides for a single tipi cover, and once they have scraped them
clean, it takes them one or two days to sew them together in a
shape like the one shown above. Women friends and relatives
usually help each other.

Men who have earned battle honours *(see page 30)* often decorate
the outer covers of tipis with pictures of their exploits, or sacred
symbols they have seen in dreams or visions.

5 Small poles are inserted at
the top of the tipi, creating
small flaps called "ears" or
"women's arms". These can be
adjusted to prevent draughts and
allow the the smoke from the fire
in the centre of the tipi to escape.
When it rains, the flaps are
closed so that the water runs
down the outside of the tipi.

INSIDE THE TIPI

All the family members live in one tipi, which makes it very crowded and allows for little privacy. As many as eleven adults and children can share a tipi, along with all of their clothing, tools, weapons and food. The lack of space makes it essential to keep things very tidy, and everything and everyone has their proper place. Brave Heart Woman and Pretty Plume Woman usually stay in the area where the food and firewood is kept and the cooking is done, while Sees the Berries Woman, as senior wife, sits at the rear of the tipi with her husband and his guests. The saddles and bridles are kept in the "men's side" of the tipi, and the men's weapons are always placed by their beds so that they can grab them quickly if the village is attacked during the night. Holy items are always placed at the rear of the tipi.

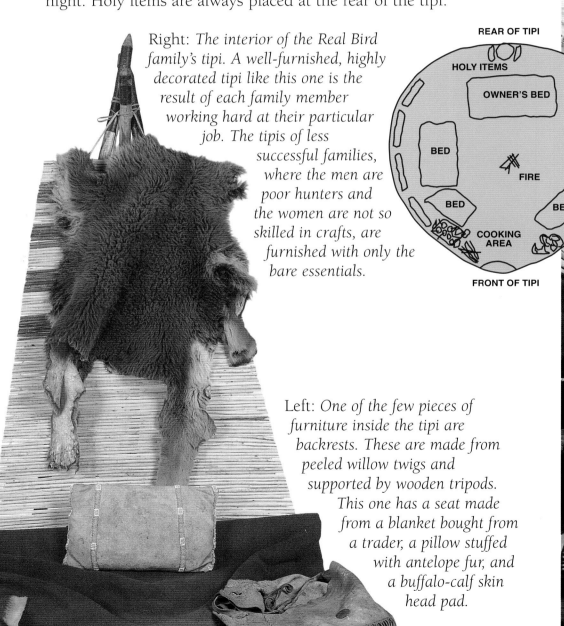

Right: *The interior of the Real Bird family's tipi. A well-furnished, highly decorated tipi like this one is the result of each family member working hard at their particular job. The tipis of less successful families, where the men are poor hunters and the women are not so skilled in crafts, are furnished with only the bare essentials.*

REAR OF TIPI

HOLY ITEMS

OWNER'S BED

BED

BED

FIRE

BED

BED

COOKING AREA

FRONT OF TIPI

Left: *One of the few pieces of furniture inside the tipi are backrests. These are made from peeled willow twigs and supported by wooden tripods. This one has a seat made from a blanket bought from a trader, a pillow stuffed with antelope fur, and a buffalo-calf skin head pad.*

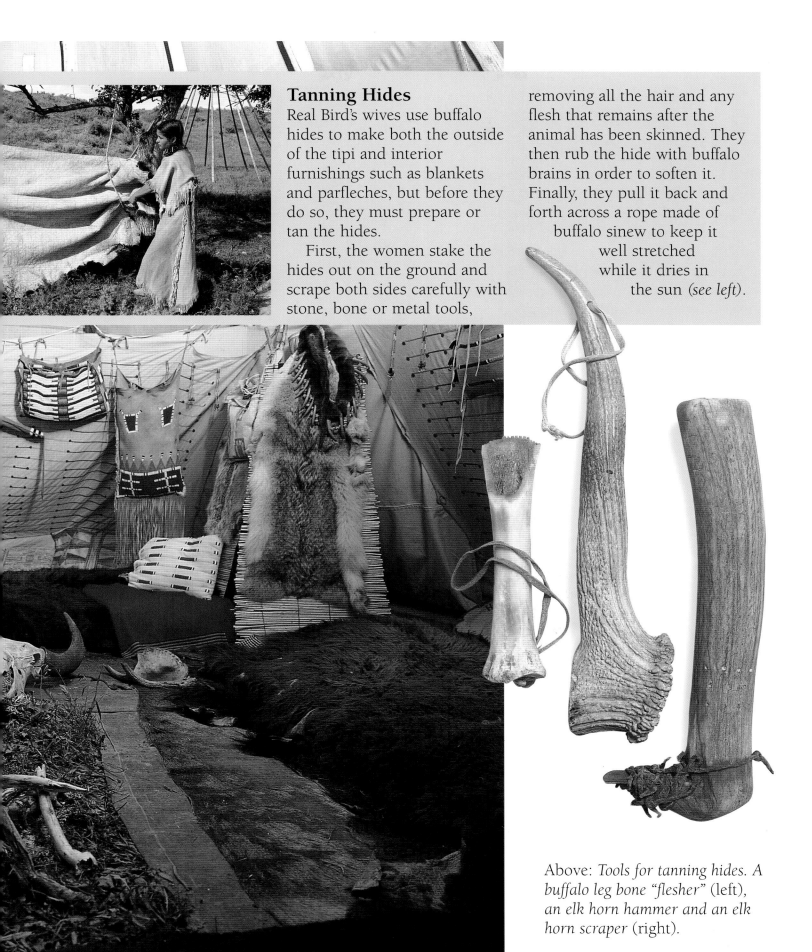

Tanning Hides

Real Bird's wives use buffalo hides to make both the outside of the tipi and interior furnishings such as blankets and parfleches, but before they do so, they must prepare or tan the hides.

First, the women stake the hides out on the ground and scrape both sides carefully with stone, bone or metal tools, removing all the hair and any flesh that remains after the animal has been skinned. They then rub the hide with buffalo brains in order to soften it. Finally, they pull it back and forth across a rope made of buffalo sinew to keep it well stretched while it dries in the sun (*see left*).

Above: *Tools for tanning hides. A buffalo leg bone "flesher" (left), an elk horn hammer and an elk horn scraper (right).*

MORNING TIME

I f Real Bird and Eagle that Sings are going hunting, or if the camp is being moved, it is necessary to make an early start. At other times, Sees the Berries Woman and Pretty Plume Woman get up first, in order to fetch wood and water, and prepare the morning meal of boiled meat and broth. Anyone who has been out the night before, feasting, dancing or visiting friends, sleeps in late, and on winter mornings everyone is reluctant to leave the warm fire in the middle of the tipi and go out into the cold.

After bathing, Sees the Berries Woman and Pretty Plume Woman oil their hair, and sometimes their bodies, with melted bear fat. They then plait their hair before they begin the work of the day. In the summer months they try to do the heavy work, like tanning hides, before the sun gets too hot.

Although some of the horses belong to individuals, including women and children, looking after them is men's work. As soon as they get up, Real Bird, Eagle that Sings and Rides the Herd go to check on the horses, take them to the river for a drink, and maybe move them on to better grass. Horses are the most important and valuable of all the Plains Indians' possessions, so Real Bird has to be constantly on the lookout for thieves. If he suspects that there are raiding parties in the area, he tells the other men to wait before moving their herds out on to the prairies to graze.

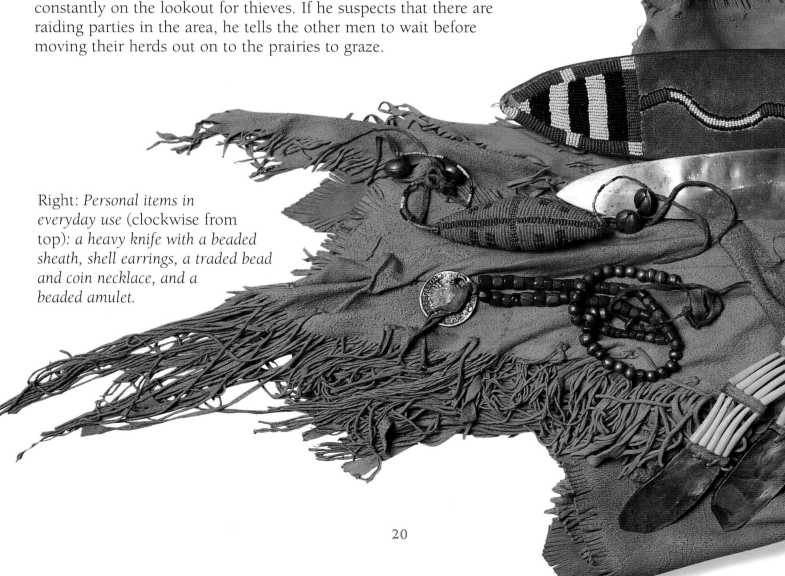

Above: *Clothes for hunting, travelling and work are simple and undecorated. Clothing for special occasions, such as battles or celebrations, is kept in beaded or porcupine-quilled saddle bags when it is not being worn.*

Right: *Personal items in everyday use* (clockwise from top): *a heavy knife with a beaded sheath, shell earrings, a traded bead and coin necklace, and a beaded amulet.*

Yucca Plants

Yuccas are used for different things: the fruit can be eaten; the spikey leaves (*above*) and outer root are used for firemaking tools; the inner root (below), when peeled and soaked in water, makes excellent soap.

Left: *Rides the Herd has a wash in the river before he goes to help the men water the horses.*

WOMEN'S WORK: FOOD

eal Bird and his family usually eat two meals a day, the
first at mid-morning and the second in the late afternoon.
These meals are prepared and served by Sees the Berries
Woman, helped by Pretty Plume Woman and Brave Heart Woman.
Like most Plains Indians, they do not grow their own crops, fruit,
or vegetables, so their diet is quite limited. Most of the food comes
from the men's hunting, but the women gather wild foodstuffs such
as berries, and barter for food with farming tribes or white traders.
They enjoy fresh meat, and the men often eat it raw at the site of
a kill. Inner organs are especially popular. Real Bird likes raw liver
with bile from the gall bladder best, but nose gristle, fresh
brains and kidneys are all favourites. The family's nomadic
lifestyle means, however, that many of their foods have to
be dried so that they can be kept and
transported from place to place. Meat and
other foodstuffs are hung up in the hot sun
until they are completely dried out and
hard. These are then soaked or boiled in
water to make them edible.

Real Bird's family has few eating
utensils. If someone is invited to a
feast, they are expected to bring their
own knife, a carved wooden bowl and a
buffalo shoulder-blade or scrap of rawhide
to use as a plate. Cups and spoons are
carved from buffalo horn. Forks are unknown,
and meat is eaten by first putting a piece in
the mouth and then cutting it away from
the rest of the lump with a knife. Meals
are usually accompanied by a drink of
water or meat broth.

Left: *Besides fresh and dried meat, there are
various other foods available* (from top to
bottom): *bitter root; a braided string of
dried prairie turnips; dried buffalo bladders
for holding water; dried corn and rings of
dried squash, both of which are
obtained through tribes who come from
the more fertile Missouri River area
further south; rose-hips (eaten when food
is scarce) set on a plate made from a
buffalo shoulder-blade; and dried
chokecherries in a wooden bowl.*

Above and left: *Pretty Plume Woman and Brave Heart Woman prepare and serve the afternoon meal.*

Below: *Women's tools for starting fires (clockwise from top left): a burning glass (magnifying glass); matches; a piece of flint; a knife in its sheaf; a bag to keep the smallest tools in, and some dried tinder. Matches, known as Lucifers because of a popular brand name, are a rare novelty on the prairies.*

23

WOMEN'S WORK: CRAFTS

G ood wives like Sees the Berries Woman and Pretty Plume Woman are skilled in many different crafts. They make all of the clothing for their family, including moccasins (*left*), as well as saddles, packing gear, tipis, tipi furnishings and various kinds of tools. Besides making everyday items, they have also mastered the traditional women's crafts, such as beadwork, painting on rawhide and porcupine-quill embroidery. They use these skills mainly to decorate clothes, since, like most nomadic peoples, the Plains Indians find this the best way to display their artistic achievements.

It is as important for a woman to be skilled in crafts as it is for a man to be a good hunter and a brave warrior. Sees the Berries Woman belongs to a special craftworker's guild for women. Only the finest craftswomen are allowed to join. Membership of this guild gives Sees the Berries Woman high status in the tribe, and the right to make certain religious items that other women are not allowed to make.

Above: *Woman's belt and knife with bead-embroidered sheath.*

Right: *Sees the Berries Woman and Pretty Plume Woman teach their daughters how to sew.*

Beadwork
The Real Birds obtain Italian glass beads at trading posts. The women string them on to threads of buffalo sinew (*above*) one at a time.

MEN'S WORK: HUNTING

As the head of the family, Real Bird's chief responsibility is to provide meat and buffalo robes, as these are the things that allow the family to have a comfortable life, with a large, well-furnished tipi and plenty of trade goods. The buffalo is therefore his most important quarry. As well as the meat and hides, every other part of the animal, from the horns to the hooves, can be used by the family in their daily lives.

Above: *Everyone needs a quirt, or whip, for their horse. For everyday use, a stick or buffalo tail will do. For special occasions, beaded wrist straps with elk horn or carved wooden handles are common.*

Right: *Buffalo with calf.*

Tools for making weapons

Almost every hunter and warrior has tools for making his own bows and arrows. It is usually older men like Timber Leader who specialise in making them because the younger ones like Eagle that Sings prefer to save their energy for hunting buffalo and will gladly trade meat and hides for new weapons.

Right:(from top to bottom): *a sharpened stone knife; stone drill (left); metal, stone and bone arrow heads (centre); a sanding stone (right); a bundle of animal sinew, and a glue stick.*

Above: *To hunt buffalo successfully on horseback with a bow and arrow, the rider needs to have good control over his horse.*

Left: *Men spend part of their leisure time making and repairing their weapons. Raw bow staves are carved into a rounded shape and backed with animal sinews to give them more power and strength. Bows can also be made from elk antlers and horns from bighorn sheep.*

Right: *Arrows are painted with the owner's individual markings so that, on a big hunt, each man can tell which animal he has shot.*

MEN'S WORK: PREPARING FOR WAR

For Real Bird and his sons, war is not only about helping their tribe capture more hunting ground or taking revenge for horse-stealing raids, it is also an important part of their culture, and has both a ceremonial and a spiritual aspect.

Men are considered to be the protectors of the tribe and are expected to help defend the village. When Rides the Herd is 13, he will begin to learn the art of warfare by accompanying war parties. He will not fight, but will fetch water, gather wood and prepare meals for the adults. When he is 17, he will be invited to join his first war party as a warrior. Young warriors like Eagle that Sings go on horse-stealing expeditions and raids until they have enough wealth to marry.

When Eagle that Sings has proved that he is a good warrior, Real Bird will be able to retire from fighting. However, like Timber Leader, he will still consider himself to be a warrior, and will always be prepared to fight to the death in order to defend the women and children in his village.

Above:
A warrior paints his horse with spiritually protective symbols and war honour marks.

Left: *The highest ranking warriors and chiefs hold a meeting in a council, or warrior society, tipi. Each man's shield is hung above his seat. In a pre-battle ceremony, the man who wants to lead a war party offers his pipe to other warriors. If they smoke it, they have accepted his leadership.*

Protective Symbols

Among the Plains Indians, representations of animals, forces of nature or the spirit world offered spiritual protection both in battle and in their daily lives. Symbols could be made from beads, quills, wood, furs or hide and then crafted onto clothes, weapons and religious items, or painted directly onto a person's body.

Below: *This paint kit contains (clockwise from centre): clamshell paint bowls and wolf moss for yellow dye; (above) buffalo-hoof paint bowl; small clamshell; three buffalo kneecap bone paint brushes; porcupine-tail hair brush; buffalo-horn powdered paint container; paint sticks; package of Chinese vermillion paint; three buckskin paint bags; three rock or earth pigments; rawhide painted case.*

MEN'S WORK: WARFARE

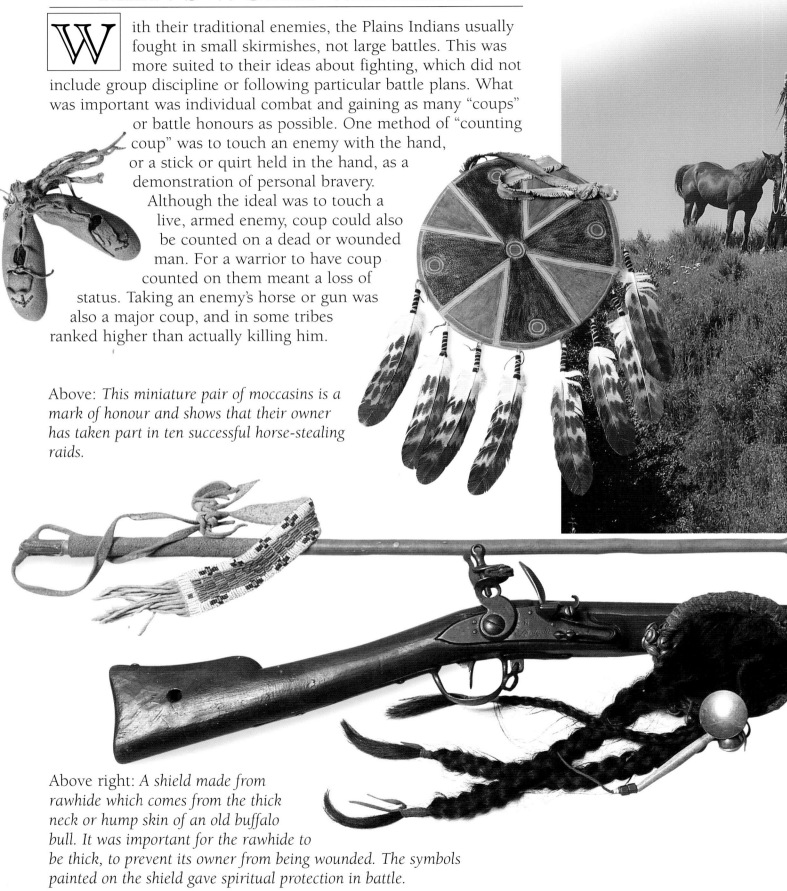

With their traditional enemies, the Plains Indians usually fought in small skirmishes, not large battles. This was more suited to their ideas about fighting, which did not include group discipline or following particular battle plans. What was important was individual combat and gaining as many "coups" or battle honours as possible. One method of "counting coup" was to touch an enemy with the hand, or a stick or quirt held in the hand, as a demonstration of personal bravery. Although the ideal was to touch a live, armed enemy, coup could also be counted on a dead or wounded man. For a warrior to have coup counted on them meant a loss of status. Taking an enemy's horse or gun was also a major coup, and in some tribes ranked higher than actually killing him.

Above: *This miniature pair of moccasins is a mark of honour and shows that their owner has taken part in ten successful horse-stealing raids.*

Above right: *A shield made from rawhide which comes from the thick neck or hump skin of an old buffalo bull. It was important for the rawhide to be thick, to prevent its owner from being wounded. The symbols painted on the shield gave spiritual protection in battle.*

Left: *The gun was the Plains Indians' favourite weapon. A sawn-off .69 calibre flintlock like this one was very effective at short range and could easily be reloaded while on horseback. Guns were often decorated, and this one is ornamented with a recently taken scalp and some of the scalp-owner's jewellery. The long-handled stone club was used in hand-to-hand fighting.*

Above and centre: *A war party. War parties usually consist of the leader, his assistants, several scouts, and some warriors. The leader of a war party carries the pipe that he has used in the pre-battle ceremony. All the warriors who have smoked the pipe during the ceremony have accepted his leadership for that particular battle.*

CHILDREN

W hen a Plains Indian baby was born, its umbilical cord was cut and dried, then sealed in an amulet bag. This represented the child's connection to his or her mother, and, through her, to the rest of the tribe and the Great Spirit. A respected relative or holy person was asked to name the child, and both boys and girls were given the names of famous ancestors or tribal heroes. A girl usually had one name, which did not change when she married, but a boy might have several different names in the course of his life, either given to him by others because of his exploits in battle, or revealed to him in a dream or spiritual vision.

Below left: *Darts and "bull roarers", which can be whirled around to make a loud noise, are favourite games amongst the boys.*

Toys and Games

Real Bird's children often play games which are an imitation of the roles that they will play as adults. Rides the Herd plays at war and hunting, and his sisters play doll's house with miniature tipis and dolls made out of sticks and scraps of cloth. Both boys and girls play ball and stick games similar to hockey or lacrosse. These games are also enjoyed by the adults.

Gambling games with counters and dice, like the one shown below, are popular with children as well as adults, who often play for high stakes such as buffalo robes and horses.

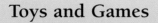

Below: *Rides the Herd and his friends play a buffalo-hunting game, using hollow buffalo hooves to represent adult buffalo, with buffalo calf hooves for the calves. Using buffalo toe bones, some of the boys pretend to be hunters and, chasing each other across the prairie, they practise the hunting skills they will need in years to come.*

Above: *While the boys play hunting games, Does Well and Two Whistles make a miniature village out of cottonwood leaves, using split twigs for the horses and travois (see page 9).*

Below: *A cut-off soldier's boot with the bottom sewn up makes a good place to keep the carved and painted sticks used in several gambling games.*

Left: *Eagle that Sings' cedar "love flute" is precious and he keeps it in a specially painted buffalo rawhide case.*

Courtship

Young warriors like Eagle that Sings spend a lot of their time in camp painting and dressing up to show off in front of the girls. After getting a girl's attention, a young man lets his intentions be known by singing flattering songs about her, or sitting outside her family's tipi for hours, playing his love flute *(top centre)*, an instrument which is believed to be able to entrance any girl its player desires.

Eagle that Sings has fallen in love with Otter Horse Woman, and has obtained permission from her family to visit her in her tipi. They stand together in the doorway, and Eagle that Sings covers both of their heads with a large blanket so that they can talk in private. Unmarried girls are not allowed to talk to men on their own, so Otter Horse Woman's grandmother, mother or aunt are always somewhere nearby.

MEDICINE

T he Plains Indians believed that everything in the world was part of one Great Spirit or "All Being" and was therefore a potential source of spiritual power. They called this power "medicine".

Amongst most tribes there were two sorts of healers, or in some cases one person filled both positions. Doctors charged a fee to splint broken bones, apply poultices, prescribe certain herbs and sew up large wounds. They often made a theatrical display in order to convince the patient of their power and to provide entertainment for his or her family.

Holy people, known as medicine men or women, used the special powers given them by the Great Spirit in dreams or visions, to attend to the spiritual needs of others.

Right: *When Timber Leader wears a bear-skin, he hopes that he will take on some of the bear's great powers of healing.*

Medicine Objects

Each person had special holy objects, such as the quilled medicine pouch, sacred stick and rattle shown here (*left*), which inspired them and helped to protect them from harm. A medicine object was not simply special because of its shape or material, but had to be made sacred by being blessed by a holy person or used in a spiritual ceremony. Everyone had their own "medicine bag" with holy objects in it. They might have seen these objects in a dream, or a holy person might have told them what to put in the bag.

Death
Dead people were dressed in their finest clothes to prepare them for their journey into the next world. Their medicine objects, food, and, sometimes, if they were male, their weapons, were wrapped up beside them in a buffalo robe. Most tribes then placed the corpse on top of a scaffold (*left*). Eventually, the bones were removed and placed in crevices in the rocks.

THE VISION QUEST

Spiritual power was usually sought in a ritual in which the person seeking aid went on a "vision quest". Leaving the village, they fasted and prayed for up to four days in the hope of receiving a sign from God. This might come in the form of an animal, bird, rock or tree, because the Great Spirit could communicate with people in any form. These visions or signs were then interpreted by a holy person.

Dreams in normal sleep were also considered to be spiritually important and a source of power, and a man might paint a symbol or animal that he had seen in a dream onto his shield, to protect him in battle (*see page 30*).

Above: A sweat lodge, built from wooden poles covered in buffalo hides and used for purification ceremonies. Water was poured onto hot stones in the centre of the lodge to create steam, and the men purified themselves physically and spiritually, by sweating.

GOVERNMENT, GATHERINGS AND FESTIVALS

Most Plains Indian tribes selected their leaders. Older men like Timber Leader served as civil chiefs, making decisions about village matters. Younger men like Real Bird were the warrior leaders, deciding when it was right to go to war. Although women's opinions were respected, they were usually voiced by their husbands.

Many tribal gatherings were combinations of social and religious celebrations, with dancing, story-telling, feasts, gift-giving, courting, speeches and games. They usually took place in the summer, when it was easier to travel and there was plenty of food for everyone and grass for the horses. Most gatherings lasted about a week, which was as long as the available grass and fuel lasted.

Below: *The pipe stem* (top) *is decorated with porcupine quills, and next to it is the carved stone pipe bowl. Below them are the beaded bag in which they are stored, bags of tobacco, a buffalo shoulder-blade tobacco board coloured with sacred red earth paint, and some pipe tools.*

Right: *Real Bird's brother, Enters the Medicine Lodge, prepares his shield and medicine bag of holy objects for a ceremony by turning them to face the sun so that they can absorb its power.*

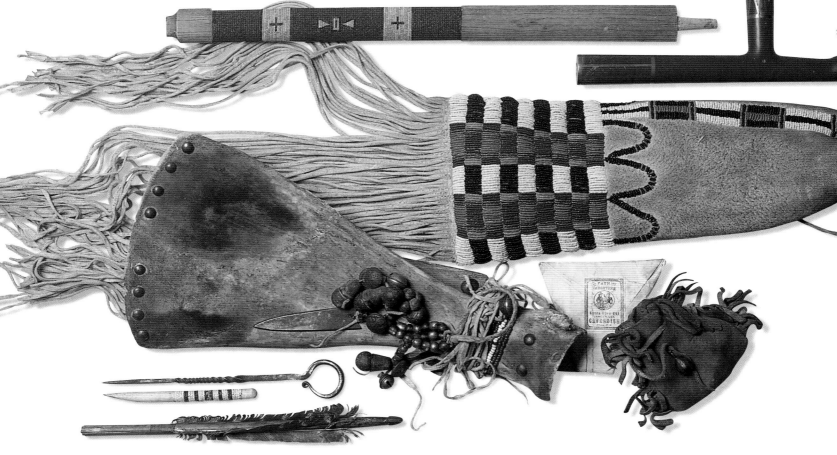

Above: *The buffalo dance is performed by men wearing buffalo head masks. It depicts a hunt and is danced when meat is scarce, in order to bring the herds closer to the village. During the dance, young men leave the village in search of the herds.*

Dances

Dancing was a very important part of the Plains Indians ceremonial, spiritual and social life. A dance could renew the earth's spirit, sustain animals and crops or revitalise the energy and lifeforce of the tribe.

Everyone was expected to dance, and both the warrior societies and the women's guilds hosted their own dances. Scalp dances, lasting many days, were held as victory celebrations over enemies.

Smoking

Pipe smoking played an important part in spiritual ceremonies. There were specially decorated sacred pipes for this purpose, as well as ordinary plain ones for social smoking. Smoke was thought to represent all the living things in the world, while the pipe was symbolic of the flesh and blood of human beings. The ceremonial act of smoking brought them together. The smoke from the pipe could represent a prayer, a gift, or a request for spiritual aid from the Great Spirit. In many tribes, it was common for both men and women to smoke a mixture of tobacco and herbs.

Right: *The piece of dried buffalo dung (top centre) is used as a sacred altar for the preparation of incense, which is made by burning sage, sweet grass or other herbs. The hollow buffalo hooves are used to mix sacred paint.*

TRADE

The Plains Indians had a long tradition of trading, both with each other and with white people. When the Plains Indians first came into contact with white traders and settlers, they soon realised that metal axes, kettles and guns could make their lives easier, and just like any other people, they liked to have new clothes and jewellery.

Horses are the most valuable items that Plains Indians like Real Bird and his family have to offer for trade. One warhorse is worth

ten saddle horses, and one racing horse is worth ten guns. A saddle horse is usually worth one gun with 100 rounds of ammunition, or eight buffalo robes. A single buffalo robe can be swapped for three metal knives or 25 rounds of ammunition, but a person who wants a gun needs to give the trader eight or ten buffalo robes. If the buffalo robe is finely decorated, it may be worth as much as three packhorses. Real Bird also offers the traders wolf and beaver fur and pemmican, which is a specific type of food made from dried meat mixed with dried berries and covered in melted fat. Pemmican is very useful to people who live on the plains because it can be kept for a long time.

Other Plains Indians traded dried buffalo meat, dried vegetables, clothing and regalia. White traders brought sea-shells and beads for making jewellery, and shell-and-bone hair pipes, such as those shown on the breastplate above. These popular accessories were manufactured thousands of miles away by white workers in New Jersey.

Some of the goods were imported from all over the world: glass beads from Italy, bright red paint from China, guns and cloth from Britain, and sea-shells from the Pacific coast and Russia.

Right: *Besides guns and ammunition, white traders would carry items such as these* (clockwise from left): *brass thimbles for sewing and decoration; tweezers for plucking facial hair; metal knives; tobacco tins; coffee; blocks of tea; packets of tobacco; matches; mirrors and "burning" or magnifying glasses for starting fires.*

Above: *The Plains Indians quickly adapted items offered by white traders to their own requirements. For example, this soldier's ammunition box and tin for percussion caps have been turned into jewellery boxes.*

Above: *This trader is well known to the Real Bird family, as he is married to a woman from their village. This often happens – the life of a trader who travels by himself is lonely, and marrying a Plains Indian woman can help to make for friendly relations with his customers.*

Above: *Brass rings from France and rings with glass stones were cheap but very popular.*

Travelling Traders

White traders travelled from village to village. Others set up permanent shops, called trading posts. During the 19th century, more and more of these were set up, especially by the fur companies, who came to rely heavily on the Indian trappers and hunters. Plains Indian men and women soon learned how to spot poorly-made goods and how to get a good deal.

LEISURE TIME

I n the summertime, almost everyone in Real Bird's village is busy with some task, construction project or with preparations for a ceremony or festival. The women are especially busy, but still manage to find time to relax by visiting friends, storytelling and playing games. Many adults stay up late, sometimes all night, attending dances and other social functions.

Winter is the time for relaxing, catching up on craft projects, and trying to stay warm and well fed while using up as little energy as possible. After sunset, the fires in the tipis are the only source of light and heat, but the beds, made of buffalo robes, are soft, warm and comfortable. The time for action will come again with the spring, when the cycle will renew itself, as it has done forever.

Right: *Both men and women enjoy gambling. Dice are made from carved bone or painted plum seeds. European playing cards, bought from traders, are also popular.*

Above: *Real Bird entertains his friends with stories of his heroic war deeds, which he has painted on a buffalo robe. This is called a pictograph, and it is one of the ways in which Plains Indians recorded their history.*

Below: *Watercolours, crayons, chalk and coloured pencils are all traded and used to make pictographs. This battle scene has been painted on a white man's business ledger.*

Above: Brave Heart Woman tells a story to her grandchildren before they go to bed. Those who have lived long lives are thought to have a lot of wisdom and it is their duty to pass on the tribal history to the next generation.

Left: *Almost everybody turns out to watch horse-racing, which is a very popular sport. Like a good warhorse or hunting horse, a fast racehorse is worth a lot to its owner.*

SOLDIERS AND SETTLERS

The nomadic, horseback culture of the Plains Indians lasted for approximately 150 years, and only during the last 25 were there open conflicts with outsiders. The first white men to arrive on the western plains were fur trappers. Known as mountain men, their relationship with the Plains Indians was usually friendly, and many learned to speak Indian languages. The Indians also got on well with the white traders, and they were able to benefit from new goods such as guns and metal cooking utensils. When the first pioneers and soldiers came, as long as there were plenty of buffalo and the newcomers did not want to settle on their land and fence it off, the Plains Indians were happy both to tolerate their presence and to engage in trade.

However, new diseases brought by the white people, such as smallpox and cholera, killed many Indians, and the white man's drink, alcohol, also took its toll. Both white and Indian hunters alike slaughtered the buffalo herds: when white men first arrived, there were about 40 million buffalo in the North American continent, but by 1890 fewer than 1,000 were left.

The white farmers who came to the plains wanted the land where the Indians had traditionally lived and hunted. During the Indian Wars (1854-1890) many of the Plains Indians were forced to move into special areas called reservations. Some of these were on their homelands, but some tribes were made to move far away to poor land which the farmers did not want.

Above right: *A painting of Fort Laramie, Wyoming, by Alfred Jacob Miller. The fort was established in 1834 by the American Fur Trading Company to buy animal pelts from mountain men and Indian trappers. In 1849 the army took it over to guard and service the wagon-trail roads that were used by immigrants and gold rushers heading to California.*

Above: *Although this photograph is called "Sunset of a Dying Race", the Plains Indians did not die out, but have adapted their culture to the modern world.*

Plains Indian Culture

This photograph shows children arriving at an Indian Training School. Schools like this one attempted to "civilise" the Indians and convert them to Christianity: the children were dressed in white people's clothes and forbidden to speak their native languages.

However, despite problems of racism and poverty, Plains Indian culture has survived: its languages are still spoken, and the Indian population of North America, which was down to 250,000 in 1900, had risen to around two million by 1990.

THE VILLAGE IN TIME

ere are some of the events that took place in American history before, during and after the period when Real Bird and his family lived on the plains of Montana.

1000 AD Norsemen make contact with the Native peoples of North America.

1492 Columbus, believing he has found a new route to China, "discovers" the New World and calls its inhabitants "Indians".

1493 Columbus returns to the New World with 19 stallions and 23 mares.

1519-40 Spanish explorers Cortez and De Soto travel and raid their way through Central America and the southern states of North America.

1600-1700 Plains of North America very sparsely populated. Eastern woodland tribes begin to obtain firearms and push weaker, unarmed tribes out of their homelands.

1720-30 Tribes venturing out onto the prairies begin to obtain horses, guns and metal utensils.

1750-60 Almost all tribes now living on the plains are immigrants from further east who have taken up the nomadic buffalo-hunting culture.

1779-81 Smallpox epidemic.

1800-30 Fur trade era begins, many animals and areas over-hunted and trapped by Indians and white trappers.

1804-6 The Lewis and Clark Expedition explores the Upper Missouri and Oregon territory.

1805-7 Zebulon Pike searches for the source of the Mississippi and explores the Rocky Mountains.

1811 John Jacob Astor establishes a fur-trading post in Oregon.

1830-70 Buffalo-hide trade era: millions of animals killed for the financial incentive of obtaining guns, metal tools, beads, alcohol and other trade items.

1830 Congress passes the Indian Removal Act, giving President Jackson the power to remove Native Americans from the east to lands west of the Mississippi.

1833 Bent's Fort built in Southern Colorado for fur trade with the southern and central Plains Indians.

1836-40 Smallpox epidemic.

1842-45 John Fremont maps the West.

1843 First wagon train crosses the continent to Oregon.

1845 John L. O'Sullivan writes of the United States' "Manifest Destiny" to expand across the continent.

1847 Marcus and Narcissa Whitman and 12 other settlers are massacred by Cayuse Indians at their mission in Oregon; the army is brought in to protect the settlers.

1848 Mexico cedes California and the Southwest to the United States. Gold is discovered in California, leading to the 1849-50 Gold Rush.

1849 Fort Laramie, a US army post, is established at old Fort William in Wyoming, a fur-trading post. Its purpose is to protect wagon train and Gold Rush immigrants.

1851 Treaty made at Fort Laramie with Northern Plains tribes, Indians promise not to attack overland routes in return for cloth, food and other amenities.

1853 Same treaty is made at Fort Atkinson with southern tribes.

Fort Riley is established in Kansas.

1854 A white settler complains that Sioux Indians butchered one of his cattle. Soldiers investigate and open fire on the Indian camp. The Indians retaliate, killing Lieutenant Grattan and 28 men in what becomes known as the Grattan Massacre. Thereafter attacks on overland routes resume.

1854 The Kansas-Nebraska Act formally opens these territories to white settlers.

1856 Smallpox epidemic.

1857-78 American-Indian Wars period: many armed conflicts between Indians and US soldiers.

1851-1880s Many treaties signed and reservations of land allotted to various Indian tribes.

1861-62 Smallpox epidemic.

1861-65 American Civil War.

1864 Massacre of Sand Creek: US soldiers kill at least 150 Cheyenne and Arapaho, mostly women and children. State of Nevada joins the Union.

1866 Fort Reno, Fort Phil Kearny and Fort C. F. Smith are built to protect the Bozeman Trail.

1866-68 Red Cloud leads the Oglala Sioux into war with the US army over the Bozeman Trail area. The government agree to evacuate forts along the trail.

1868 Real Bird and family are living on the plains of Montana.
Fort Laramie treaty of 1851 is re-negotiated. Lands contested between the US government and the Lakota given to the Lakota.

1869 First American trans-continental railroad is completed.
The Battle of Summit Springs, Colorado. The power of the Southern Cheyenne Dogmen is broken.

1871 Fort Abraham Lincoln is built in North Dakota to protect railroads.

1874 Fort Robinson is built in Nebraska to watch over the Lakota reservations.

1876 Battle of Little Big Horn: Sioux and Cheyenne warriors defeat General Custer's troops.
State of Colorado joins the Union.

1877 Chief Joseph of the Nez Perce surrenders to the US Cavalry.
Crazy Horse of the Oglala Lakota surrenders and four months later is killed resisting arrest.

1878-86 The last of the great buffalo herds are destroyed and with them the 150-year period of the mounted Plains Indian culture.

1881 Sitting Bull of the Hunkpapa Lakota surrenders.

1887 Buffalo Bill's Wild West Show performs for Queen Victoria in England.

1889 Two million acres of Indian territory (Oklahoma) are opened to white settlers.
State of Montana, North Dakota, South Dakota join the Union.

1890 Battle of Wounded Knee: end of the American-Indian Wars.
Sitting Bull killed by Indian police.
States of Idaho and Wyoming join the Union.

1896 State of Utah joins the Union.

1899 State of Washington joins the Union.

GLOSSARY

Amulet A small religious item, like a charm, which has spiritually protective qualities. The Plains Indians wore amulets in their hair, on their bodies or attached to their clothing or horse harness.

Buffalo robe A tanned buffalo hide with the hair left on to give it extra warmth. Robes were used for bedding and swapped for trade goods.

Cottonwood A large hard-wood tree used in the construction of saddles, bowls, clubs and many other items. The bark from the upper branches was used as food for horses in winter.

Elk A very large member of the deer family found in the western states of America.

Flintlock A front-loading gun used by many soldiers and Indians in the 19th century. When a flintlock gun is fired, the flint strikes an L-shaped piece of metal called a frizzen and makes a spark. This ignites the gunpowder in the gun's pan and causes the powder inside the gun to explode, firing the shot.

Great Spirit One of several names for the supreme deity worshipped by the Plains Indians. Other names were All-Being, Mysterious One, Grandfather and Old Man.

Medicine Holy power. A medicine man or woman is someone who is known to have this power.

Nomads Peoples who have portable homes and roam from place to place over a large area, looking for food and grazing.

Parfleche Any untanned or rawhide material folded to make a bag or carrying-case, from a French word meaning to parry, or turn an arrow.

Pictograph Stylized drawings painted in pigments (*see below*) on tipis and clothing to record battle feats or successful hunts.

Pigment A natural or man-made substance used for colouring or dyeing clothing, tipis and horse equipment. Plains Indians applied pigment to their skin both in the form of decoration and to help prevent sun-burn.

Prairie The large, grassy level or slightly rolling area of land of the Missouri-Mississippi valley. It has few trees, but rich soil and enough rain for growing grain crops. On its west side, the prairie merges with the high plains, where lack of rain makes the land more suitable for grazing animals than growing crops.

Rawhide An animal hide that has been scraped clean on both sides (flesh and hair), and then stretched and dried to a semi-rigid consistency.

Reservation An area of land set aside for use by specific Indian tribes or nations.

Scout A guide. Scouts, who knew the land well, travelled ahead of hunting or war parties, looking for the quarry (eg. buffalo herds) or the enemy. They then reported back to the party's leader.

Settler In the 1850s and '60s, pioneers, also known as "overlanders", left settled parts in the east to go and build new homes in the west, which was only just being acquired by the US government. They travelled in large groups, in a line of covered wagons known as wagon trains.

Sinew Animal tendons used as thread for sewing, binding and repairing various items.

Tipi A conically-shaped, portable tent made of buffalo hides, elk hides or canvas. (A wigwam, sometimes confused with a tipi, is a bark-covered hut.)

Travois An A-shaped apparatus made of poles of wood. It was attached to a horse's back and used to haul heavy loads.

Yucca A large plant with stiff, swordlike leaves branching from a central stalk. It was used for firemaking tools and for soap. The soft, nut-flavoured seed could be eaten.

INDEX

Places to Visit and Useful Addresses

AMERICAN INDIAN TRUST
66 Gloucester Road, Brishopston, Bristol BS7 8BH
Telephone: (0117) 9426437

THE AMERICAN MUSEUM
Claverton Manor, Bath, Avon
Telephone: (01225) 460503

THE BRITISH MUSEUM
Great Russell Street, London WC1B 3DG
Telephone: (0171) 636 1555

HORNIMAN MUSEUM
London Road, London SE23 3PQ
Telephone: (0181) 699 2339

NATIVE AMERICAN EDUCATIONAL TRUST
21 Little Preston Street, Brighton, BN1 2HQ
Telephone: (01273) 328837

THE PITT RIVERS MUSEUM
Parks Road, Oxford, Oxfordshire OX1 3PP
Telephone: (01865) 270949

Acknowledgements

Breslich & Foss would like to thank Kennard Real Bird, Jack Real Bird, Jim Real Bird, Henry Real Bird, Ramona R. Real Bird, Shawn Real Bird, John Real Bird, Mark Real Bird, Polly Real Bird, Lucy Lee Real Bird, James Real Bird, Sloane Real Bird, Jessi Real Bird, Terry Anna Cummins, Nicole Cummins, Kordell Cummins, Brandon Yellow Wings, Hartford Lee Bear Claw, Tiffany Glenn and Roy Martin for acting as models and for the use of their land and their horses.

Picture Credits
Thomas Gilcrease Institute of American History and Art, Tulsa Oklahoma: pp.4-5 (bottom).
Glenbow Archives, Calgary, Alberta: p.4 (top right), ref. NA-936-34.
Joslyn Art Museum, Nebraska: pp.42-3 (top centre).
National Anthropological Archives, Smithsonian Institution: pp.42-3 (bottom centre), p.43 (top right).
Princeton Collection of Western Americana: p.43 (bottom centre).

All clothing, regalia, tipi furnishings and horse equipments made by Michael Bad Hand Terry, except: tipi interior, pp.18-19, beaded moccasins, p.24 and paint bag, p.28, by Roy Martin; large grizzly bear claw necklace, p.31, by John Arrasmith; and painted rawhide bags pp.15, 31, 39 and 40, by Ivan Hankla.

Village set technicians and assistants: Jason White Dog Terry and Silas Sky Mentzer.

Landscapes, tipi interiors and artefacts were photographed at the Little Big Horn Battlefield site at Gerryowen, Montana, USA.